STEP INTO MY POWER

JAMIA WILSON ★ ANDREA PIPPINS

WIDE EYED EDITIONS

CONTENTS

INTRODUCTION

Do you remember a time when you felt powerful?

Illustrator Andrea Pippins remembers stepping into her power when she ran for the role of sixth-grade class president and won. She felt like her ideas and voice mattered when she heard her classmates' interests for the school year and wove them, along with her vision, into a campaign and community events.

Similarly, I felt powerful when I had opportunities to speak my truth during my youth. I'll never forget the sense of purpose I felt when I was first asked to recite my poetry at a church conference. I reflect on this moment when I need a reminder that my voice is, and always has been, a megaphone that I use to change hearts and minds, and advocate for justice.

Both Andrea and I know first-hand that learning how to own and use our power as girls and young women helped us realize our dreams. We understand that the world can be tough to navigate at every level, from handling conflicts with friends, family members, and bullies, to dealing with politics, inequality, sickness, hardships, and having to obey rules you inherited or aren't old enough to vote for or against.

That's why we'll be exploring what it means to know and trust our insights and capabilities with stories, images, activities, resources, and action prompts that you can interact with on your own time and, most importantly, on your terms. No matter where you are, *Step into My Power* is here for you with caring advice and actions you can take and make your very own. It's an invitation to take steps, big leaps, or small tip-toes toward your goals. This book is a celebration of the fact that you are entirely enough as you are, but might need encouragement while reaching for your goals. It's here to be your unconditionally loving friend or even an imaginary sibling if you're an only child like we are.

You are not alone, even if it feels that way sometimes. Think of this book as a paper-bound GPS that can help you navigate your thoughts and feelings. Whether times are joyful, rough, or somewhere in between, *Step into My Power* will always have your back. Although you already possess all you need inside of you, we are here to reassure you every day, every week, and every month that you are enough, and you have what it takes to turn your vision for your life into action.

— **Jamia Wilson & Andrea Pippins**

POWER

YOU'VE GOT THIS!
Tap into your strengths

SLAY YOUR FEAR!

TELL THE TRUTH:
Saying "Yes" to saying "No"

STAY INTACT:
Hold on to your wholeness.
You are enough.

KEEP CALM:
You belong! Take your
rightful place

DEFINE YOURSELF:
Write your own life rules

YOU'VE

tap into your strengths

HAVE YOU EVER FELT LIKE YOU'RE NOT SURE WHAT YOU'RE GOOD AT, OR THAT THE THINGS YOU DO WELL DON'T MATTER AS MUCH AS THE WAYS OTHER PEOPLE SHINE?

When I was younger, I used to feel that way. I wasn't an expert ballerina or award-winning swimmer, like some of my friends, and I was in a school that valued physical achievement.

I didn't see my unique gifts as assets when I was growing up. Teachers and parents made me feel bad about things they prioritized, such as being a whiz at algebra, and playing tennis (which flared up my asthma and ignited my anxiety). I sulked about not fitting into the mold people in charge expected of an otherwise "good" student.

GOT THIS!

Instead of embracing my talents, I quietly beat myself up for not being a perfect child who was skilled at everything I tried. Whenever my father, or a teacher would say, "But you're so smart, you are not working up to your potential in math, or Arabic class, or 'fill-in-the-blank with something I'm not a genius about'," my breath became shallow. I knew deep inside that I learned differently when it came to numbers, and although I wasn't as quick at math, my talent for word problems in the same math class would later help me achieve my dreams as a writer when I grew up.

I share this story because I walked around with a secret for many years. I hid behind my sunny smile and felt ashamed that I had to have a tutor to help me with Mathematics, due to my visual disability and the challenges that came with it.

INSTEAD OF FORCING MYSELF TO BE SOMEONE ELSE'S BEST SELF, I'D WRITE MY YOUNGER SELF THIS LETTER ON MY FAVORITE STATIONERY:

Mia,

The world would be boring if we were all good at the same things. Don't beat yourself up for not being perfect. Take time to listen and hear what people ask you for help on, and compliment you about. What aspects of who you are, are you most proud of? What do folks appreciate about what you share with them, and most of all what stirs your soul so much that you never look at your watch when you're doing it—because therein lies your answer—and follow it.

Love,
Your Older Self

P. S. Oh, and … Keep reading and writing. It will help you find your purpose.

⊙➡ STEP INTO YOUR POWER

Imagine you are older;
write a love letter to yourself
right now...

Speak to yourself with the
same gentle and generous
spirit you would use to address
a very small child.

Pay attention to the courageous
whispers from your heart, and
less to the roar of critique from
the world around you.

You are impacting the world in your own special way.

Recognize your natural abilities and passions and urge yourself to keep going with them – even if not everyone values them with the same weight you do.

Although I'd love to meet the small percentage of humans who have never experienced dread or angst at some point in their life, the reality is that most of us are—or have been—afraid of something.

As someone whose family once nicknamed her "worry wart," it can be challenging to confess my fears to people who might judge the things that stir me up—like the stage fright I still experience every time I speak in public (even though I do it often, and for a living). But I'm facing my fears and calling on you to join me. Let's get to know your concerns, understand their roots, and end our shame so we can share our unique gifts with the world.

Once I learned that our amygdala (the fear center of the brain), is triggered whenever we feel something is threatening, it helped me make sense of whether this small, two-centimeter region of our brain is telling me the truth, or making a mountain out of a molehill.

This "fight or flight" response can be useful when there's a hungry tiger chasing us down the street—it makes us panic and run! But things like performing in a school talent show can set off similar spinning thoughts, restless legs, sweaty palms, feelings of doom, or however it personally shows up for you. These physical responses can make the two feel eerily similar.

THAT'S WHY I'M SHARING SOME OF THE TIPS I'VE USED ALONG THE WAY THAT HELP ME SLAY THE FEAR-TIGER THAT TRIES TO CHASE ME DOWN EVERY TIME I MOVE TOWARD BEING BRAVE.

⮕ STEP INTO YOUR POWER

FIRST, INTRODUCE ME TO YOUR FRENEMY, FEAR.

Make a name tag for Fear. Write down who they are, where they are from, where you first met them, and what they look, smell, and sound like. Sketch them out on a piece of paper. If your Fear is a shadowy shape-shifter, make a list of all of their alter-egos and aliases. Once you write them down, thank Fear for all you've learned from them and then ceremoniously bid them farewell by ripping up the paper.

Now that you've taken a courageous step, it's time to make another one. Former American First Lady Eleanor Roosevelt once said,

"You gain strength, courage, and confidence by every experience in which you stop to look fear in the face."

Her words are often misattributed to say "do one thing that scares you every day," which I took to heart and added to my calendar as a daily prompt. When I wake up, I write down "today's bold move" in my calendar every day. Depending on the day it varies from "be honest about your need for solitude or space" to "go to a group class at the gym" (which brings this bookworm back to panic about having to play mandatory team sports in high school).

What's your bold move today or this week? **DO IT. I DARE YOU.**

TeLL THe TRUTH:

"WHAT'S THE WORST THING THAT CAN HAPPEN?"

is a question I've learned to ask myself when I struggle with simply saying one powerful two-letter word, "no." In almost every instance, the reality of what might happen if I set a boundary that is healthy, is not as terrible as the cost of not being true to myself.

One of my first memories of my battle with "no" occurred when my Grandma asked all of my girl cousins to help wash Christmas dinner dishes, while our male cousins were allowed to play games. As a spunky seven-year-old, I was annoyed that these boys, who had the same abilities, weren't expected to do housework. I was told off for being selfish when I said,

"No, I won't wash these dishes unless they do it too."

SAYING "yes" TO SAYING "NO"

I'll never forget what it felt like to be given the cold shoulder from the boys for the rest of the evening and, most of all, to disappoint my Gran.

Although I'd always been taught to say "no" when faced with unfairness, I learned that people don't always practice what they preach.

From then on, I felt pressure to be a people pleaser. These messages were supported by demands from parents, teachers, friends, and what I observed about the backlash that sometimes happens when girls and women say "no" on TV.

There's an important difference between drawing a line in the sand in order to focus on your priorities, versus saying "no" to be purposefully unhelpful, shirk on promises, or wriggle out of taking responsibility. That's why it took years for me to realize that saying "no" had nothing to do with me being mean or difficult, and everything to do with claiming my power.

ONCE I LEARNED TO UNDERSTAND THAT STATING "NO" MEANS SAYING "YES" TO MY DREAMS AND VALUES,

I BEGAN TO UNDERSTAND THAT "NO" IS A POSITIVE TOOL.

NO

You're invited to use **"no"** as a complete sentence at least once this week, without apology. Your **"no"** can take many forms, and the way you do it is up to you.

HERE'S A ROADMAP THAT MIGHT HELP YOU:

Say no to burning yourself out to get someone else's approval.

Say no to other people's judgments about who you are.

Say no to negative self-talk and forgive yourself.

Say no to a habit that is no longer serving you. For example, once my food allergies were identified, I stopped eating food that made me sick to be polite.

Say no to fear, and tell your fear who is in control: you.

Say no to something that feels like an obligation (unless it's homework or a promise you've already made) and choose inspiration instead.

Say no to _____.
(Choose your "no!")

The burden of other people's expectations can feel stifling. I know first-hand that this is easier said than done. We live in a culture that pressures us to have it all, be it all, and do it all while supporting everyone but ourselves.

Let's embrace Chimamanda Ngozi Adichie's wisdom that,

"there are people who dislike you because you do not dislike yourself."

Recognize that setting healthier boundaries in our lives is a massive step toward caring for ourselves on a deeper level. It's worth the price of a few naysayers who may not have learned these lessons themselves yet.

STAY INTACT:
HOLD ON TO YOUR WHOLENESS. YOU ARE ENOUGH.

**"DO YOUR HOMEWORK."
"TRY HARDER." "HAVE YOU DONE
YOUR CHORES?" "SECOND PLACE?
NEXT TIME LET'S GO FOR FIRST."**

Sound familiar? Growing up, I spent a lot of time focusing on being liked and seen as a "good girl." From Sunday school to the classroom, I absorbed the message that my worth was related to what I could do for others and how hard I worked. It took ages for me to realize that although being of service is meaningful, it is being—not doing—that defines human dignity.

No matter where we are on our path or how many times we stumble, we are enough. In a society that sometimes tells us we are broken for being less-than-perfect, it can be easy to forget that we are, by our very nature, intact.

I was reminded of this when I saw my favorite soul singer, the late Nina Simone, perform at a grand concert hall in Washington, DC. As Nina sang, "When you feel really low, there's a great truth you should know / When you're young, gifted, and black, your soul's intact," the diverse crowd rose to its feet and echoed her words:

NINA
SIMONE

"your soul's intact, that's a fact."

She permitted us to see ourselves as <u>whole</u>, to claim our value, and to remain rooted in who we are during change or hardship.

THROUGH NINA'S MUSICAL SCHOOLING, I LEARNED OUR PURPOSE IS TO BE TRUE TO OURSELVES.

Recognizing the marvelous yet straightforward power of our existence helps us access a sense of peace and internal knowing. That's why I try to close my eyes, sit quietly, and breathe into my questions or worries. It reminds me that being here is strength in itself when times are tough. Breath shows us that the most critical part of us is working, and the rest can always be figured out.

⮕ STEP INTO YOUR POWER

Pick your favorite quiet place and sit in a comfortable position. Place your hand over your heart, close your eyes, and breathe. Next, visualize your future self. Imagine being so confident in who you are that no one else's views about you or ideas about your role are a factor. Pay attention to your mind and body.

Is it easy to see yourself and your worth without considering negative or positive input from others? Or, is it hard to think about who you are without hearing other people's voices of praise or critique? What does it feel like to be free of other people's expectations? What sensations are stirred up or disappear when you imagine your intact self on your terms?

Next, draw an image of yourself based on what you pictured during your meditation.

KEEP CALM

YOU BELONG! TAKE YOUR RIGHTFUL PLACE

What does "belonging" mean to you? For me, it's about having a strong sense of self so that no matter what place you are in, you are rooted in your birthright, purpose. We all deserve to be secure in our identity.

Even though we live in a comparison-driven culture, we're all bonded by our common humanity. Although we may receive messages to the contrary, or have more or less access to status, no one of us is more valuable than the other.

To be sure, it is easier said than done to feel like we belong when we're in an environment with people who we share few things in common with, or when we're left out of group activities because we're new or different. That's why we must practice checking in with ourselves and understanding the strengths we carry with us. This way, when something happens that moves us away from feeling comfortable in our own skin, we will be our own North Star, and bring ourselves back to the heart of our being.

We humans develop a lot of our ideas about who we are and where we fit in from our friends, family, and the people we spend time with the most. We often share similar beliefs to the people nearest to us, which can have a positive influence, but sometimes makes us more close-minded or restless about trying new things and meeting new people.

While being a part of a group can help us discover who we are and teach us how to collaborate, we can be negatively impacted in spaces where we are isolated, pressured by our peers, or expected to conform to unrealistic standards.

Since our social groups play a big role in impacting how we perceive ourselves in positive and negative ways, it is vital for us to be clear about which habits and beliefs are our own, and what we've adapted to fit in.

When I need help showing up in my fullest truth and realness, I think of my singer-songwriter friend, Morley's song, *Be the One*. She sings,

"IT'S ALRIGHT, TAKE YOUR RIGHTFUL PLACE ... FEEL YOUR POWER IN THE WAY YOU DO WHAT YOU DO. BE THE ONE TO FIND A WAY OUT OF NO WAY. BE THE ONE TO OPEN DOORS AND STAND HEAD HELD HIGH, STAND IN POINTED PLACES, AND MAKE THEM ROUND."

Her words always remind me to respect the groups I'm in, and to respect my truth by being sincerely myself. When I need to be reminded of the power I possess, I hum her tune about how finding belonging within helps us make a difference.

WHAT WORDS OR PICTURES REMIND YOU OF YOUR POWER AND BRING YOU BACK TO CENTER?

STEP INTO YOUR POWER

If you don't have a motto yet or an image that brings you back to your core self, take some time to explore possibilities. Think about keeping these words and pictures close to you so they are always there when you need them.

When I need a pick-me-up or am feeling insecure in a new social setting, I often refer to a small wallet card I made that is etched with Maya Angelou's words:

"You alone are enough. You have nothing to prove to anybody."

NINA SIMONE

DEFINE YOURSELF:
Write your own life rules

"**Follow the rules.**"

Chances are, you've heard these words countless times. In school and at home, rules can provide us with instructions that help keep us safe, organized, principled, and on the same page with people in our community. Additionally, rules can also

Pelé

inform how we participate and measure our progress in sports, math, school elections, and everything in between.

Although rules can benefit us and teach us valuable and necessary lessons, they are also capable of being flawed, biased, one-sided, or outdated. Whether they are spoken or unspoken, rules can become habits and practices born from expectations that no longer fit the needs, diversity, and realities of our current society.

Pushing the limits of traditional boundaries can inspire creativity, expand imaginations, offer fresh perspectives, or influence new standards within an industry—like the famous Brazilian soccer player, Pelé, known for his unique "ginga" footwork, or the one-of-a-kind style of the classically-trained pianist, jazz singer and songwriter, Nina Simone. From Dr. Martin Luther King, Jr. to surrealist Mexican artist Frida Kahlo, trailblazing advocates and artists throughout history have shown us that there are times when not following "the rules," or coloring outside the lines can help change the world. Although King and Kahlo are well-known examples of this, many other dreamers and everyday heroes display the faith, leadership, and courage it takes to ask themselves and others who made the rules we're supposed to follow, how those rules could be improved to represent the wide-ranging diversity of humanity, and what they could do to offer new, more just and visionary ways of being and doing.

IN THAT SPIRIT, I CHALLENGE YOU TO THINK ABOUT THE RULES THAT GUIDE YOUR LIFE AND ASK YOURSELF WHICH ONES ALIGN WITH YOUR VISION AND PURPOSE, AND WHICH ONES DON'T. WHAT OLD RULES NEED TO BE LEFT BEHIND, AND WHICH NEW NORMS NEED TO EMERGE FOR THE TRUEST YOU TO SHINE THROUGH?

DR. MARTIN LUTHER KING, JR.

Frida Kahlo

STEP INTO YOUR POWER

On my sixteenth birthday, my family gave me a framed plaque of Colin Powell's short-but-sharp "Rules of Leadership." (Colin Powell was the first African-American to be appointed as US Secretary of State.) Although my family supported a different political party, they respected and valued his wisdom.

When I met Mr. Powell years later, I had an opportunity to share how much his rules have taught me (especially his sage words: "It Can Be Done.") As I rushed to express my gratitude quickly, while snapping a selfie of our time together, I thanked him for motivating me to create my own life rules.

Based on his example, I made my own list that is always expanding as I learn from life's highs and lows. The rule on the top of my list is:

"Define yourself. Or, somebody else will."

What rules need to be created or rewritten in your life? Take my advice and define your own rules at the scale (ongoing, short-term, long-term) that works for you.

MY RULES

1.

First, sit down in a quiet place or a space with calming music. Then, close your eyes, put your hand on your heart, and listen to the whispers of your soul. You may call this reflection, meditation, or whatever feels right for you. Listen to what comes up for you and honor it without judgment.

2.

Next, write down a list of current rules in your life (set by others or yourself) that are holding you back from your wishes and goals. Ask yourself how these directions came into being, why they became habits, and whether there is anything you can do about transforming them to create the possibilities you're dreaming.

3.

Then, write a journal entry that includes the origin story of the rules that don't work for you, and explore whether they are yours to own, or if they were passed down by others but might not fit into the plans you have for your life going forward.

Journal

4.

When you're done, think about what you might do to help you sharpen your connection to what really stirs your heart and mind. For example, you may be part of a family where you feel pressured to try out for sports teams because everyone is an athlete, but you really want to focus on developing your artistic talent. Identify which rules in your life are ones you have adopted because of other people's expectations and which ones feel like they belong to you, your values, and your passions.

5.
Next, write down a list of
your very own rules and
illustrate them with collages,
doodles, or other forms of
expression that suit you. Don't
forget that we can dream big
while taking small deliberate steps to
help us reach our aims.

6.
If some of the "outside" rules you're dealing with
are fixed and beyond your control, think about what
choices you have the power to make. This allows
you to set intentions that help you feel closer to
navigating life with your own compass every day.

7.

Finally, draw a personal coat of arms. Don't worry about being fancy or official. Choose the colors, shapes, values, natural elements, and motto that define you on your own terms. Once it is done, every time you're pushed to follow the crowd in the battle to be yourself, envision this crest as an imaginary shield you can wield with your spirit, actions, presence, and voice. My personal crest depicts two dreadlocked mermaid lionesses with a chevron, which is a symbol for protection.

IT READS: FAITH. WISDOM. COURAGE. LOVE.

Community

LIFT AS YOU CLIMB:
Support your squad

FIND A MENTOR:
Learn from your heroes

ASK FOR HELP (Especially when you need it most)

LIVE AND LET GO:
Dealing with drama, bullies, and fickle "friends"

LIFT AS YOU CLIMB

support your squad

Has a story ever etched itself onto your heart like the names of two friends carved onto a tree? When I was ten, *Hope for the Flowers*, an illustrated book about caterpillars moving through life's changes and growing as a result of collaboration became my holy text. A school librarian recommended Trina Paulus' brightly colored book to me when I asked for a book that explores the meaning of life.

If you haven't read it yet, it's about Stripe and Yellow, two caterpillars seeking out their life path by trying to move up to the top of an endless tower of other climbing caterpillars. Along the way, they discover that stepping on other caterpillars and climbing to the top is not the key to transformation, and they choose to collaborate, take the risk of spinning cocoons, and to emerge as butterflies, together.

Growing up, I thought of this book often when faced with social pressure to compete against other girlfriends instead of supporting them. A few years later, I remembered it when the most popular boy at school told me that I would be banished from sitting at the much-desired lunch bench we called "the table" if I didn't stop talking to people he thought weren't cool enough for our crew.

Instead of playing into his game, I decided to invite several of the girls he wanted us to shun to join us. When the boy who I'll call "Jack" gave me a nasty look and hissed that he was warning me, I said he could keep the table and that I'd be taking my new friends and all of the cupcakes I'd baked for everyone over to a bench. As I was walking away, one of the girls asked me if I was sure that I wanted to risk losing my place at "the table."

IT WAS THEN
THAT I KNEW
THAT I WAS
MOVING
INTO MY OWN
TRANSFORMATION,
AND THAT I
WAS TAKING A
LESSON FROM
MY BELOVED
CATERPILLARS
BY CHOOSING TO
FLY TOGETHER
INSTEAD OF
DIVIDING AND
CLIMBING.

STEP INTO YOUR POWER

I'm proud to know Ann Friedman and Aminatou Sow, two pals and authors of the book *Big Friendship*, who have taught me a lot about how to support your squad.

They created the term and idea of "shine theory" which they define as:

❝I don't shine if you don't shine. ❞

In a society that often pushes girls to compete, diminish, or undermine each other's talents, "shine theory" urges us to expand through supporting one another. The way I understand this is that "if I win, you win" and vice versa. There's enough room for all of us to rise to the top and we're even stronger together.

Reach out to a friend and ask her how you can support her with a dream she's been holding on to. Tell her one thing every day this week you have noticed about how she shines brightly. Finally, if there's someone you admire but have been shy about approaching, reach out to her this week with a compliment, a kind note, or an offer to hang out.

FIND A MENTOR:
LEARN FROM YOUR HEROES

Three years ago, my partner Travis was driving through New York City, when he brought up an interesting conversation he once had with a great jazz musician:

> **"You can learn how to read music and play an instrument in school, but there's nothing as powerful as creative community and really listening to the masters of their craft."**

Those words made me think about the people who moved me to find my ideas and voice: quirks, occasional self-doubt, meandering expression, and all ...

In my life, I have learned from three women—Lauryn Hill, Nina Simone, and Erykah Badu. I've learned from studying their approach to their trade, and the way that they embody their work.

Learning life lessons from your role models is about trying on some of their traits for yourself, like being brave, speaking up, leading a group activity, or doing something different from the norm.

Once you identify the characteristics that inspire you, see which ones fit with your soul. This isn't about copying or comparing yourself to another human. It's about seeing someone reflect the power and abilities you already possess. As simple as it might sound, I've come to believe that there is a Lauryn Hill or Erykah Badu song that deals with most of my trials and worries. Sometimes, when I'm feeling stuck or beaten down, and can't find the answers within myself, I imagine how the women who inspire me would respond to the situation. Erykah would tell me to breathe, "pack light" and hold on to myself. Lauryn would tell me that "respect is just a minimum." Even though I'm not a singer, these songstresses have taught me that what I do in the world is just as much about how I be.

Their soulful courage and sense of unconditional self-love (in a culture that often fails to recognize women of color's worth and power) moves me. Each of these women has earned mainstream success while staying true to their values.

Their openness about themselves showed me that they have also struggled. It struck me that no matter what imperfections they revealed, I regarded them as powerful, wise, and beautiful—regardless of impossible standards of beauty, life difficulty, and other challenges. They made me feel heard, recognized, seen, and understood.

I used to beat myself up for falling back into unhelpful patterns or shrinking myself to make other people feel comfortable, while my heart screamed that I should be bold.

I REALIZE NOW THAT ALL THE FALLING, CRAWLING, AND GETTING BACK UP ARE PARTS OF MY STORY.

○ STEP INTO YOUR POWER

Think about who your life muses are. Depending on your dreams, these might be leaders in the arts, sports, politics, history, science, travel, entertainment, food, environmental, or literary worlds. Think about what you want to learn from these masters of craft, even if you never get to meet them. While their writings, ideas, songs, art, poems, or performances may be representations of themselves that inspire you, think about their

presence, expression, and the way they move in the world. Learn from their lessons about embracing who you are and accepting or even celebrating your shortcomings.

I have a feeling that if you do this, someday you'll be someone else's inspiration.

ASK FOR HELP

ESPECIALLY WHEN YOU NEED IT MOST

> "Help me if you can, I'm feeling down, and I do appreciate you being 'round, help me get my feet back on the ground, won't you please, please help me?"
>
> —The Beatles

What comes to mind when you think about asking for help? In elementary school, my friend Sarah held weekly Beatles-inspired dance parties in her apartment. Without fail, we'd dash around the den singing at the top of our lungs.

Today, I remember all of the lyrics to the songs we learned by heart. But, one tune surfaces when I'm overwhelmed, stressed, or hurting. The song "Help!" became one of my anthems because its harmonious and relatable lyrics remind me of what it feels like to be supported and accepted. It taught me that asking for help (and giving it, too) is a normal and healthy part of life.

Some people will tell you that asking for help is a weakness. Some of my family and faculty

members at school certainly told me it was a flaw. But the Beatles' sunshiny song acknowledges that everyone needs help, and honors how common it is for people to need encouragement and companionship to feel more content, confident, and secure.

If you're someone who struggles with asking for help, especially when you need it most, it's nothing to be ashamed of. We live in a culture where talking about finding and accessing support can be easier said than done. In a media climate that thrives on superhero stories about exceptional people, it's common to feel ashamed that our lives don't feel as effortless and straightforward as other people's might look on TV or in the glossy pages of your favorite magazine.

That's why it's vital for us to understand that offering help and receiving it are a key part of both strengthening relationships, and living well throughout our lives.

For those of us who find it easier to help others than to accept support from someone else, we must remember what they teach us every time we fly on a plane:

"PUT YOUR OXYGEN MASK ON FIRST, BEFORE HELPING OTHERS."

STEP INTO YOUR POWER

Whether you need a boost or ongoing support, you are not alone, even if it feels that way sometimes. From asking your parents or guidance counselor for a tutor if you need to improve at school, to inquiring about summer classes to catch up after failing a course, there's no shame in taking action to get what you need to thrive. This also applies to your life outside of the classroom.

If you're troubled by bullying, fear, overwhelmedness, stress, sadness, worry, self-harm, extreme changes in your appetite or eating habits—or anything else—some people will have your back. While it can provide great comfort to confide in your friends, it's essential to seek advice from a trusted adult who can help you get what you need.

Nervous about asking the people closest to you for support? Consider reaching out to a counselor at school or a therapist if you're having difficulties in your relationships with family, friends, or other authority figures. If you have peer educators or coaches in your community, place of worship, or school, connect with them to gather information, build bonds, and learn about resources.

In most cases, it is good to partner with your parents or guardians on engaging a counselor. If you don't feel safe doing this, ask your potential therapist these questions directly to help inform your decisions:

• Do you have experience working with people from my community/culture/background/religion/age?
• What are your legal obligations regarding parental involvement and consent?
• What are your confidentiality guidelines for minors?

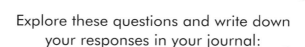

Journal

Explore these questions and write down
your responses in your journal:

1. "How does a (relationship/situation/
challenge/person) make me feel?"
2. "What makes me feel supported?"
3. "What would feeling better look and
feel like for me?"
4. "What needs to change for that to happen
and what can I do to move it along?"

Practice sharing what you write down with
a parent or other dependable adult or a
trustworthy friend who may be
able to lend a hand.

RESOURCES OUTSIDE OF SCHOOL

• Need urgent support? No matter what you're facing, *Crisis Text Line* provides 24/7 private counseling and support via SMS messaging. Text 741741 anonymously from anywhere in the United States to connect with an active listener who will help you with problem-solving and a wide range of resources.

• For questions and support about racial equity, visit the *Kellogg Foundation Resource Guide* online. It lists programs across the United States.

• Have questions about your body or relationships? Schedule an appointment with your local *Planned Parenthood*'s teen program to talk with a peer educator or health coach.

• To access LGBTQ+ support in the US, contact the *It Gets Better Project*. You could also visit *The Southern Poverty Law Center* website, which fights hate groups and bigotry using education, litigation, and advocacy. They have resources you could share with a teacher about how they can best serve LGBTQ+ students.

• For gender equality, health, and the well-being of girls and women, visit *Women Deliver* online.

• To access support about immigration, join the *United We Dream* network online. They are the largest immigrant youth-led community in the United States.

Don't forget, you can also set up your own organization if you can't find one that exists. There will be plenty of people out there thinking the same things as you.

LIVE AND LET GO
Dealing with drama, bullies, and fickle friends

Do you believe in ghosts? I know I do, but not the kind that we dress up like for Halloween. I'm talking about fair-weather friends who only appear during times of good fortune and become hard to get ahold of when you need help. Or, frenemies who look and act like friends one day, and then treat you terribly.

My first memory of a soured friendship goes back to first grade. Although I was one of a few black students in a mostly white class, I never felt left out until the day one of my classmates invited the entire class to her birthday party, except for me. Since we played together every day, I figured she must have forgotten to add my name to the guest list. I imagined every other response than the mocking words that spewed out of her mouth in front of a crowd, "Mom doesn't like blacks because she says you guys are bad. I don't want to be your friend anymore." My encounter with discrimination and betrayal left an imprint on my heart. For years, I thought of how sick it made me feel every time someone picked on me. I needed to be a friend to myself by facing my feelings, releasing shame, and taking steps to build connections with people who share my values.

Discovering how to let go of relationships that hurt more than they help is challenging. It takes time to realize that our personal feelings, actions, and responses are ours to own, and we're not responsible for other people's inability to return generosity or love.

RELATIONSHIPS MAY SHIFT BUT WILL ALWAYS RESULT IN A LESSON.

Whenever I would introduce a new friend to my mother, she'd say, "Friends come into your life for a reason, for a season, or for a lifetime, which one do you think this one is?" It was her reminder to focus on how I want to show up in the world versus the outcome I want from others. Although we can't control people's behavior, we can focus our energy on setting boundaries and modeling the deeds we want to see in the world. Since experts agree that friendships with people who celebrate our goals and support us boost our well-being, it's important to invest in them.

CONNECTIONS WITH FRIENDS WE CAN GROW WITH DIMINISH OUR STRESS, GIVE US A SENSE OF BELONGING, AND STRENGTHEN OUR SELF-CONFIDENCE.

⊙ STEP INTO YOUR POWER

Take stock of the people you interact with the most on a daily basis.

Ask yourself the following questions:

1. Is my energy level high when this person is around?

2. Are they usually supportive?

3. Do they give as much as they take?

4. Do they apologize when they have made a mistake? Do they support me when I have made mistakes?

5. Is my energy level low when this person is around?

6. Do they often belittle, criticize, name-call, or judge me? Do I associate this person with the negative voice in my head?

7. Do they make me feel like I have to be someone other than myself to be their friend?

8. Do they try to pressure me to do things I don't want to do?

If you answered yes to 1–4, consider writing notes of appreciation to the people in your life who support you, and write down qualities they possess that inspire you and how you approach friendship.

If you answered yes to 5–8, these relationships are either unhealthy, draining, or need improvement. Think about whether you feel comfortable talking with them about what needs to change or whether you'd feel happier if you moved on. If so, it's time to refocus your energy on your passions and bonding with folks who uplift you.

If you are experiencing stress, anxiety, or abuse, keep a trusted adult informed and talk to a counselor about coping tools and ways to heal.

CHOICES

**TAKE HEART AND
TRUST YOUR GUT**

ASK FOR IT:
Own what you want

DON'T FIT IN?
Pave new ground

**BE YOU,
NOT "PERFECT"**

TAKE HEART

TRUST YOUR GUT

Do you ever struggle with making decisions? The good news is that we come equipped with a compass that tells us what to do: our gut. Like all animals, we humans use our instincts to cope with changes, determine direction, protect ourselves, and survive. Our internal GPS is a navigation tool that our ancestors have relied on for centuries. While reason and critical thinking are important and should inform our actions, we're often taught to ignore the power of our intuition, which is often commonly referred to as **"trusting your gut" and "following your heart."**

While gut feelings aren't fail-safe and can be confused by bias, genuine mistakes, and hasty judgments, they can help us deepen our awareness about our surroundings, improve with time and experience, and provide valuable knowledge through lessons learned in the past. Although our guts can't speak to us in English, they communicate in another native tongue: through nerve signals to our brains and our tummies.

Our instinct is our inner voice and it is important to pay attention whether it whispers or it roars. As someone who considers herself a highly sensitive person, I always bristled at the limitations

of the quip "feelings are not facts." Although I love logical evidence, we often just "know" when things are wrong because our bodies tell us so.

Have you ever seen someone trying to copy off of your paper in school and it made your stomach hurt? Or have you ever felt uncomfortable because you have been asked to keep a secret that you know could get you or someone else in trouble? Do you ever feel like you don't want to hug a stranger even if you're being encouraged to do so? The icky "uh-oh" reactions you might feel in your body and mind are signals that something is off.

OUR BODIES POSSESS A WISDOM THAT CAN HELP GUIDE US, HEAL US, AND PROTECT OURSELVES. TUNE IN AND LISTEN.

→ STEP INTO YOUR POWER

No matter whether your situation is related to safety, or if you're mulling over a decision, it's important to listen to your intuition because it serves us best when we give it plenty of practice.

HERE ARE A FEW PRO-TIPS ...

- Write a list of three times you listened to your gut or followed your heart

- Next, write three times you wished that you followed your intuition but didn't. Jot down what you learned.

- Outline your body on a piece of paper. Label what feelings you experience and where when you're excited, fearful, anxious, nervous, overwhelmed, tense, comfortable, or content.

ASK FOR IT:
OWN WHAT YOU WANT

I was born a diplomat. Or, at least this is what my parents said when they joked about my natural negotiation skills.

Years before I even understood what the word "negotiation" meant, I was clear about what I wanted, who might help me achieve it, and often, how it might result in helpful outcomes for others.

Whether I was appealing to my parents about extending my bedtime so I could read my favorite books for longer, or bartering with shopkeepers over whether they could lower their "best price" at my local market, I discovered that I felt most powerful when I embraced my urge to ask for more. Once, I owned my power by questioning a teacher who graded me less than male schoolmates on a group project where I did most of the work. I challenged him and said I wanted our grades to reflect our efforts equally—and after some initial discomfort and a frank conversation about my contributions to the project, it worked.

Although it was awkward to confront an adult about something thorny, my respectful but direct approach resulted in a positive change. Also, it opened his eyes to the fact that he was focusing attention on who had the loudest voices during our presentation, without regard for who put in hard work behind the scenes.

What I learned from these experiences is that a world of possibility exists between a firm "yes" or "no." Unless we speak up and ask, we may never know if we could have had more options. To be sure, it is wise to use our best judgment when choosing when to push these limits, and it's most important to respect rules that prevent people from getting harmed or left out.

With that said, despite receiving mixed messages from adults about directly communicating my wants and needs, I understood deep down that I felt most powerful when I honestly expressed what I needed.

Even if it doesn't always turn out the way I hope, I have never regretted living by this motto, *Qui audet adipiscitur*, which translated from Latin means **"she who dares, wins."**

Sam A

Jamia C+

Mike A-

GRADE BOOK

STEP INTO YOUR POWER

HAVE YOU EVER HELD YOURSELF BACK FROM ASKING FOR WHAT YOU WANT?

If yes, is it because you're afraid of being labeled "bossy" or being excluded? I can guarantee from my experience, that staying in the shadows or keeping silent won't help you get closer to your dreams.

TAKE THESE STEPS:

1. Get to know yourself. Is there something about your own self-talk that is making you doubt your worth? If so, work on building up your confidence.

2. Ask for what you want every day this week, and do so without apologizing, looking down, or avoiding eye contact.

3. Let go. If you meet criticism, awkwardness, or the silent treatment as a response, it doesn't mean your request or you are the problem. In fact, it could be someone else getting used to a shift in the power dynamic or merely being unable to meet your need. Don't take it personally, accept my congrats for being true to yourself, and take the lesson with you.

DON'T FIT IN?

When I was 18, I enrolled at university to study my passion, broadcast journalism. Whenever CNN flashed on the screen, I pictured my future self: an award-winning global journalist and fearless front-line correspondent like my childhood idol Christiane Amanpour—except with long kinky braids and brown skin.

Then, something shocking happened. My teacher, an older white male professor, peered down at me through his glasses and said, "I'd hate to see you waste your articulateness. You are well-spoken, have a young face and you'll enjoy a long shelf-life in the media field, but you'll have to straighten your hair in order to be taken seriously in media." As if that wasn't bad enough, he went on to challenge me to identify "one black woman with [natural] hair like yours on a major media network" to prove his point.

My stomach churned when I heard someone I looked up to tell me that I would need to change myself, my appearance, and the hair type I was born with to be on camera. I knew that my ideas and my mind were more important than the texture of my curls. Still, it hurt to be told that my voice would not matter unless it was packaged in a body that fit a very narrow beauty standard.

Years later, when I was asked to represent my job on a major TV network, I thanked this professor for driving me toward my media activism, publishing, and public speaking work.

Pave New Ground

Although our interaction was initially painful and unjust, it taught me a valuable lesson. Now, instead of asking myself what I need to do to be included, I wonder what I can build to pave new ground without shrinking myself. My professor also taught me that just because someone else might underestimate you it doesn't mean they are right.

IF THEY MISUNDERSTAND YOUR POWER, IT'S THEIR LOSS, BECAUSE AS LONG AS YOU KNOW THAT YOU CAN DO ANYTHING YOU SET YOUR MIND TO, YOU'RE ON THE ROAD TO VICTORY.

STEP INTO YOUR POWER

My friend Carolyn often says, **"Don't give away your power,"** when she sees me or others listening to naysayers instead of owning our own abilities, skills, talents, and value.

Make a pledge to yourself to write down what power you do have and what you can build or create with it next time you find yourself in a situation where someone or something makes you feel like you don't belong.

Next, take what you write and turn it into an action plan. Jot down the following prompt.

This month I will take these three steps toward chasing my dream. Maybe you're good at art. Make it happen by committing to draw for at least 15 minutes a day; drawing your own version of a Google doodle and applying for their annual contest; and starting your own Instagram feed featuring your original designs. (Check with an adult first before joining social media sites.)

BE YOU, NOT "PERFECT"

Throughout my life, I have seen how the media impacts how we see ourselves, our voices, and our bodies. I remember growing up and having my parents sit me down at dinner to "de-program" me when I wanted to straighten my hair so I could have a silky side-pony tail like girls I saw on TV instead of an afro-puff, or wondering why in Saudi Arabia where

I grew up as an ex-pat, some of my schoolmates focused on looking like US and European TV stars, bleaching their skin and hair, and shrinking themselves in order to fit a narrow vision of beauty. It seemed to me that the pressure to fit into "the mold" drained so much energy that could have been channeled into joy.

It was disturbing to see so much focus being put on girls' looks instead of our views, from the movie theater to magazines, and even in school and athletics. Author and activist Gloria Steinem taught me that **"the trouble is that women in the media are treated like ornaments and not instruments."** I understood that there was nothing wrong with me, or us. Instead, the problem was with the system and culture that has been teaching girls and young women that we have to be perfect or contort ourselves into everyone else's vision of who we should be instead of ourselves.

Sadly, since you live in the same world I'm inhabiting, I'm sure you've encountered similar pressures to do everything right, excel while making it look effortless, look put-together all the time, and do it all with a smile at some point in your life.

That's why I'm here to say, let's bid farewell to all of that. Perfection doesn't exist, and that's a good thing. We're not robots. We're living, breathing, thriving organisms that are always growing and evolving in all of our pain, beauty, curiosity, vulnerability, and strength. You never need permission to be yourself. You don't need to look like anyone but yourself; you don't have to define yourself by other people's judgments; and your hunger does not need to be ignored.

THE TRUTH IS, EVERY ONE OF US IS PERFECTLY IMPERFECT,

**AND
THAT'S WHAT
MAKES US
DIVERSE
AND
EXCITING.**

STEP INTO YOUR POWER

Tell a friend everything you love about who she is and how she shows up in the world.

Tell her about all of the things you appreciate about her and how her actions, ideas, unique quirks, and skills impact your life.

HAVE FUN WITH IT!

Later, write in your journal about what it felt like to share your observations about this person. Imagine what it would feel like to talk to yourself in the same way when you're feeling pressure to be anyone but your stunning, singular, one-of-a-kind self.

ACT

SPEAK TRUTH TO ADULTS:
Know your rights and take action

DON'T AGONIZE, ORGANIZE:
Create what you need

IN A RUT? GET UNSTUCK!

BRANCH OUT:
Find your crew

SPEAK TRUTH TO ADULTS

KNOW YOUR RIGHTS & TAKE ACTION

Do you ever feel like adults tell you what to believe more often than they ask for your opinion? Studies show that our thoughts about policies, governments, and power, are influenced by our closest relatives. That's why it's important to educate yourself about your rights, stay up to date on current events, and determine what inspires you.

Although we don't always hold the same viewpoints as our family, our upbringing may shape our political ideas over

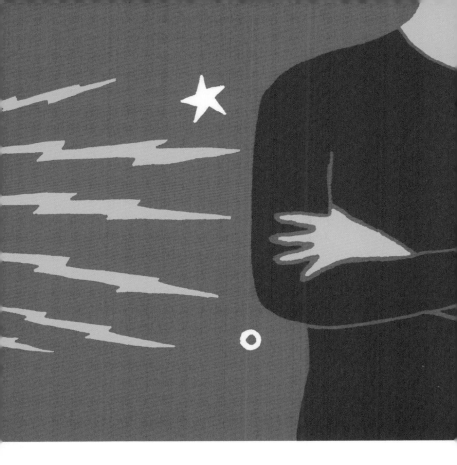

time. If your parents push you to adopt their perspective, they may influence your beliefs in the future. Even if you rebel as a kid or teenager, in adulthood, people generally return to the political leanings they were raised with.

People often argue without remembering that most of us want similar goals—**freedom, justice, safety, and personal choice.** The tricky part is that people often hold different visions about how to achieve those goals.

It's okay to disagree with the people we care about and to trust our own feelings as our ideas evolve. We're all impacted by the culture and systems we live with, but the solutions we envision for the world's problems may be different from our parents or friends.

For some, the existing structure comes with benefits, and for others, setbacks. That's why it's important to learn as much as you can about the laws, policies, and cultural norms that impact your community and beyond. Once you know what matters most to you, you can take part in changing what needs to be fixed.

If you're prepared with basic information about how your school, community, or government works, you're in a better position to achieve the progress you're seeking.

It's always a good time to understand how to support yourself and your values.

YOU DON'T HAVE TO WAIT UNTIL YOU'VE BEEN MISTREATED, WITNESSED INJUSTICE, OR WANT TO CHANGE A RULE, TO EDUCATE YOURSELF AND MAKE YOUR VOICE HEARD.

○ STEP INTO YOUR POWER

HERE ARE SOME WAYS YOU CAN TAKE ACTION:

Congratulations! You have been elected leader of your country for the duration of this exercise. Write or record the speech you would give to your citizens.

Read the **UN Convention on the Rights of the Child** to understand your rights as a young person. Consider joining Model United Nations or your school debate club.

Regularly read your local newspaper, and one from abroad, to understand timely topics from diverse perspectives. You can also do this via news sites, streaming, podcast, and radio news shows.

Explore your legal rights and your local constitution via a civics class, and through online research.

Practice speaking up in the ways that feel right for you. This could be via blogs or vlogs, creating or signing petitions, or making zines, documentaries, or posters.

DON'T AGONIZE, ORGANIZE
create what you need

Do you ever feel like the weight of the world's injustices is so heavy that it's hard to figure out how to take action? Don't worry, it's normal to feel overwhelmed by a chaotic political landscape and a media cycle that never sleeps.

Although it can be tempting to curl up and hide when we see a problem that needs fixing, we always have the power to choose to take a stand. I learned this from my parents who grew up in the segregated Southern US during the 1960s.

My mother's memories about her involvement with rallies and teach-ins during high school and, most of all, her story about marching on Washington with Dr. Martin Luther King inspired me. I asked her repeatedly to tell me about what she felt while she sat-in at segregated lunch counters, or registered voters in spite of pressure and unfair punishment.

Years later, my activism was born on the playground when I told off bullies for taunting other kids. I participated in my first anti-racist protest at the age of 10 with my parents. Some of my classmates had nicknamed me "Rebel with a Cause," and I lived up to it. I set up recycling campaigns at school, ran for class president, and passed petitions to fight apartheid in South Africa.

When I studied the women's rights movement in the sixties a few years later, I learned about the late black feminist firebrand Florynce "Flo" Kennedy, who said, "The biggest sin is sitting on your [bum] … Don't agonize. Organize." Her legacy and call to action continues to resonate with the rising tide of resistance worldwide.

We all benefit from supporting each other's right and access to free speech, assembly, and media that help us make informed decisions about our lives.

While it can be intimidating when we're not able to find the "right" words, or the absolute best approach to making a difference, being a part of the solution is more important than perfection. Why? Because if not us, me and you, then who?

EVEN IF YOU LIVE IN A PLACE WHERE IT IS DIFFICULT TO FIND PEOPLE WHO SHARE YOUR VIEWS, OTHER FOLKS IN THIS WORLD BELIEVE IN THE CAUSES YOU CARE ABOUT AND HAVE YOUR BACK.

STEP INTO YOUR POWER

GIVE BACK

protest

write letters

VOTE

POPULAR CULTURE MOVES HEARTS AND MINDS AND PLAYS A MAJOR ROLE IN SHAPING OUR ATTITUDES.

Choose a past or present movement that interests you and discover as much as you can about it through reading activist biographies and memoirs, and watching documentary films online or in the library. Next, create and share a political poster, zine or political newsletter, infographic, meme, podcast, or vlog about what you've learned.

Integrate your interest in activism into your schoolwork. Do a presentation about what you've learned and how you can apply it to a current or local issue you would like to take on. Consider joining an existing group or club focused on activism at your school, community center, or house of worship. Or, start a new campaign with your friends or other like-minded people.

IN A RUT?

Get unstuck!

Have you ever felt like you're living in a real-life quicksand scene from a cartoon? Or, do you ever feel like you're running on a treadmill with no end in sight? If so, you're like me, and many other humans who have at some point in our lives felt stuck.

Sometimes we're up against the wall of ourselves, and it's hard to imagine a better future than what's in front of us. Whether you're clinging to a bad habit, feeling under-motivated, or keep criticizing yourself after making a mistake, it can be hard to rise out of, around, under, or above a stubborn rock of a rut.

In some cases, there are real challenges in our way that prevent us from moving forward. We're often held back by our fear of losing control, a lack of confidence, or feeling overwhelmed by pressure or judgment from the people around us. Mostly, our doubts about the real power we do have in the face of difficulty contribute to us getting in our own way. Since it took me many years to learn to spot how I might be playing a role in holding myself back (even in the face of solid challenges) I thought I'd save you some time and hopefully some hard-fought lessons.

Although this book is too short for me to list all of the times I've had to crawl, push, dance, and march my way out of mental potholes that prevented me from understanding how to own and harvest my abilities and insights, I thought I'd share the two questions I ask myself when times get tough.

"NOW THAT I CAN SEE I NEED TO FIND A SOLUTION, WHAT DO I HAVE THE POWER TO DO?"

AND "WHAT CHOICE DO I HAVE THE POWER TO MAKE?"

STEP INTO YOUR POWER

IN A SLUMP?

First, know your value. You matter, period—not because of what you do, but because of who you are.

Then, see it for what it is and say out loud,

"I see you for who you are. I accept you, and like everything else, this too shall pass. I choose to let you go and claim my power."

I know this might sound silly, but ruts are bullies, and we never back down from those.

Next, make a list of baby-steps you can take to get closer to your goal and write them down or type them into your planner.

Finally, move your body and shift your mind. When I'm feeling stuck, I jump on my trampoline, do mood-boosting method workouts that combine dance, positive affirmations, and martial arts, hold a dance party of one in my living room to shake off stuck energy, or take a walk in the park before returning to my writing, cleaning, drawing, French class homework, or other projects I've put off.

BRANCH OUT: FIND YOUR CREW

Do you ever wish you had more people in your life who understand and support you? Despite all of the buddy flicks and squad shows on TV, finding friends we can rely on can be easier said than done. Whether you have a ton of friends you've known from the start, or you're feeling lonely because you've started attending a new school, it can be tough to open up and build new relationships. But, stepping out of your comfort zone to meet folks who fascinate and encourage you, can broaden your outlook and enrich your life.

If you're interested in making new connections or need a support network with hobbies, and goals that match yours, reach out. Opening up and interacting with people outside of your inner circle can be scary but it almost always delivers positive results.

Working with Andrea Pippins on *Young, Gifted, and Black* and now, *Step into My Power* has affirmed my belief in branching out. If we hadn't reached out to each other many years ago, we would have missed out on a beautiful partnership that is still growing.

JAMIA WILSON

ANDREA PIPPINS

BY LETTING GO OF
CLOSED-OFF CLIQUES
AND MAKING YOUR
FRIEND GROUP
INCLUSIVE, YOU EXPAND
YOUR EXPOSURE
TO NEW SKILLS,
CULTURES, AND
IDEAS. IT'S A GREAT
WAY TO EXPERIENCE
ACCEPTANCE,
BELONGING, AND
RECIPROCITY, AND
IN TURN, OFFER
THAT FEELING TO
OTHERS.

STEP INTO YOUR POWER

DO YOU HAVE TROUBLE INTRODUCING YOURSELF?

Here are a few short phrases you can practice while making eye contact, standing or sitting up, extending a smile, and offering a handshake—if it feels appropriate. People love compliments, so don't be afraid to share if you've heard about their talent or unique skills or interests too!

• "Hi, my name is _____, I'm in_____ school / class and I'm really interested in learning about the _____club you organized. It's nice to meet you. How are you?"

• If you've heard about them through a mutual friend, or you have other common ground or connections, mention it to break the ice. "I've heard wonderful things about you and your singing from our mutual friend Rachel! My name is _____. Nice to meet you!"

• After you introduce yourself, start out by asking your new friend questions about their passions. Listen deeply, make eye contact, and avoid distractions like looking at your phone. You're paving the way to discover common ground.

• Be aware of body language and non-verbal cues. Humans do a lot of our communicating through our bodies. If you notice that someone is keeping a bit of distance or not comfortable with hugging or touching, respect their boundaries and don't take it personally.

• Practice telling your personal story, so you're ready when you're engaging new people. I use leadership expert, Marshall Ganz's "story of self, story of us, story of now" framework to help me create a narrative of my life that reflects my values and passions. By telling your own story, it will also inspire your new pal to share their own.

1. The "story of self" helps you introduce who you are as a person—an artist, an advocate, a student, a volunteer, an athlete, etc.

2. The "story of us" gives you a chance to say how you or your passion relates to what you're trying to do in school or the community or the world.

3. And the "story of now" is telling a new friend about why you're passionate about X or Y, and providing a takeaway about how they can get involved.

WHERE TO FIND YOUR GREAT NEW FRIEND:

• Join an organization that empowers girls. Organizations like Girl Scouts, Girl Guides, and the Radical Monarchs, an activist organization for girls of color, organize opportunities for young women to learn skills, participate in cultural and educational activities, collaborate, and lead.

• Go to camp. Camp is a great place to find your squad (and make new pen pals if they live far away) because everyone shares a common experience of being in a new environment and trying new adventures.

• Follow your interests. Go to a music centre or sports club to find people with shared interests.

• If funding is a concern, some sleep-away and day camps offer scholarship programs to help with the cost, and others are sponsored by charities who offer tuition for free. Ask your school or teacher for more information.

• Follow up. If you've met someone new on a field trip or outing with your school, be sure to reach out afterward to let them know you enjoyed meeting them. Make sure to mention something you remembered about your time together or a common experience you shared, and invite them to stay in touch.

SELF-CARE

BE KIND TO YOURSELF

LISTEN TO YOUR BODY

DEALING WITH ILLNESS

FIND THE LESSON:
Bounce back from the dumps,
failures, and other bummers

**SHINE BRIGHTLY WITHOUT
BURNING OUT**

Be Kind to YoURSelf

For me, few words have left my heart throbbing more than something my friend Kathleen said one day when I was speaking about a tough time I was going through.

At the end of my rant about the volcano of stress I was feeling, she said, "Wow. The way you talk to yourself is far too harsh. You're kind to everyone but yourself. Give yourself a break. It doesn't have to be this hard. Breathe." Does this sound familiar?

At the time, I was startled by the force of the truth she shared. But I listened to her advice and took a deep breath … I was embarrassed that my friend had seen me so clearly, and angry about feeling exposed. At the same time, I knew she was right. For as long as I can remember, I have wrestled with slaying the dragons of my expectations. I realized I had cared for others, but not for my own body and spirit. As someone who has lived with a disability my entire life, I spent so much time uncomfortably pushing myself to adapt so I could be "normal" that I lost sight of the fact that everyone is entitled to self-care— including me, and including you.

After my conversation with Kathleen, I attempted to write down my thoughts for a few hours. Now that we'd had this conversation, my mind was swirling with what I took as criticism, and I burned with shame, sadness, and fear that something was wrong with me because I wasn't practicing self-care as well as the people around me.

Sometimes our harshest critics are in our own heads.

I realized that this pattern of thought was a textbook example of what Kathleen described. At that moment, I acknowledged that her comment collided with my fears of being hurt or cast out. Fears that came from past experiences with bullying and encounters with discrimination. We all encounter self-doubt from time to time, but it was painful to hear someone else comment on my own struggle with negative thoughts.

Once I allowed myself some quiet and space, I realized where and when I had been taught to be unkind to myself. Only then was I able to face reality, and start taking steps to change my relationship to my most reliable and enduring friend—myself.

SOMETIMES THE
PEOPLE YOU LOVE
SEEM TO SEE YOU
MORE CLEARLY THAN
YOU DO YOURSELF.
THIS ALSO MEANS
THEY CAN SAY THINGS
THAT CUT TO
YOUR CORE.

➡ STEP INTO YOUR POWER

If you're stubborn like me, you might need to hear why being kinder to yourself can make you more helpful to the people you adore. If you've been on a plane, you'll remember how the flight attendants instruct you to put your oxygen mask on first before helping others. I often think of this message when I'm feeling overwhelmed, notice pain in my body or anxiety in my mind.

Try writing in a **gratitude journal** every day. It can help you treat yourself the way you aspire to treat others: with kindness and love. Before I go to bed, I write down everything and everyone I'm grateful for.

When I wake up the next morning, I write down an affirmation for the day. One of my statements is: "I let go of yesterday; I embrace today. I am enough, and I have what it takes." What's yours?

LISTEN TO YOUR BODY

Do you trust your body, your longest faithful friend? Our bodies heal, protect, and move us through our lives, but we don't always take time to check in and pay attention to what's happening inside of us.

It's important to tune into our body's messages to hear what it needs. We can then pinpoint and address challenges before they become a problem. In turn, we can also discover what feels good so that we can give our bodies more of what makes them flourish.

Whether it whispers hints through gut intuition, or roars in the form of discomfort or pain, our bodies are designed to work for and with us every day. Since we're often moving swiftly in a fast-paced world, we can forget everything our body does for us until something goes awry. My body always lets me know that she ultimately calls all the shots. As someone who has wrestled with long-standing health issues throughout my life, I've learned to listen to the hints my body offers and take them seriously. When something feels out of order, it's time to observe our body's signals so we can provide the food, sleep, rest, water, fresh air, or other support it requires. Alternatively, when something like yoga soothes me into a place of peace, it's a reminder that my body responds positively to relaxation and stretching.

eat

ALTHOUGH WE ALL HAVE DIFFERENT BODY TYPES, SIZES, COLORS, AND SHAPES WE ALL BENEFIT FROM UNDERSTANDING OUR BODY'S UNIQUE VOICE, AND GIVING IT THE MOVEMENT, TRANQUILITY, STRETCHING, OR SUPPORT IT NEEDS.

drink water

meditate

STEP INTO YOUR POWER

- **Check in with your body.**

Take time to concentrate on your body throughout the day. Notice what you're feeling in your gut, your joints and in your back. Do you feel clenched or at ease? Do you notice these symptoms arising in certain spaces or around specific people or situations? If so, talk to a trustworthy adult about connecting with a therapist.

- **Jumpstart each day.**

Need a little jolt to wake you up in the morning? Do ten jumping jacks or hop on a mini trampoline to kick-start your energy and release tension. I do this whenever I start a writing project and need a surge of creativity.

journal

exercise

- **Keep breathing.**

Next time you feel tense, uncomfortable, tired, or jittery, take a deep inhale in through your nose. Next, push your right nostril and exhale out of the left side of your nose. Follow this by inhaling with the left nostril and then pushing on it while you exhale through the right nostril. Afterward, swap nostrils and alternate between them. If you feel silly, do it in a private space. This breathing practice comes from yoga.

• Lay it out.

If you need to wind down after a busy day, lie down flat on your back in a quiet space. Close your eyes. Imagine yourself releasing anything that feels heavy, stressful, or worrisome into the ground below you. Picture yourself sinking closer to the Earth, vertebra by vertebra, until you feel more peaceful. Envision all of the stress melting off of your body in the form of imaginary seeds that fall to the ground and will re-emerge as new energy in bloom.

• Catch your ZZZs.

If you're always tired or feeling exhausted throughout the day, try sleeping at the same time every night and waking up at the same time every day to train your body. If you have trouble resting through the night, ask a trusted adult to take you to the doctor for more support.

- **Talk about it.**

If you're feeling under the weather or experiencing symptoms of discomfort, soreness, or pain, reach out to a dependable adult and a healthcare provider you trust for help. Put prevention first and get help sooner rather than later to ensure the best outcome.

- **Keep your energy up.**

Always eat breakfast to ensure that you can get-up-and-go without crashing later in the day. If you feel yourself moving slowly, or feeling listless, feed yourself protein-rich snacks and water to stay nourished.

DEALING WITH ILLNESS

Do you live with a chronic illness? I do. Over the years, I have slowly accepted the fact that my body is sensitive and requires extra attention to self-care. Instead of being distressed about the fact that it functions differently than others', I've shifted my focus toward how it has expanded my sense of what matters most in my life.

After years of apologizing and feeling guilty for something that is out of my control, I have embraced that my body is my ultimate spiritual teacher. She's a perfectly flawed teacher who forces me to listen to the messages I'm getting from aches and pain, to drink water like a mermaid, and to cherish sleep as if it were holy, because it's the minimum my body needs to prosper.

For me, acceptance is not giving up. I can't say that having an illness of any kind is easy or fun, but I can say that managing treatment in partnership with my doctors and caretakers, and developing coping strategies gets better with time. While I'm not a doctor or nurse, I know how it feels to feel vulnerable and frustrated when your body won't cooperate with your plans.

Being tired or sick does not define you or anyone else, even if it sometimes feels that way. Illness is a part of the human experience and it is never your fault. If you've just been diagnosed, you might feel uncomfortable, scared, or disappointed. It's perfectly normal to process feelings that arise or to want to have time to think about your situation before talking about it. It is hard to comprehend how difficult a health condition can be until you have one. But, I have a greater respect for what it takes for people to get out of bed, show up, follow through, and create things when they are managing an illness. I also understand that above all else, taking the time and space you need to heal your body is more important than anything else.

THAT'S WHY I'M SHARING WHAT I'VE LEARNED TO HELP ME OVERCOME FLARE-UPS, OVERWHELMEDNESS, SLUGGISHNESS, STRESSFUL DOCTOR'S VISITS, AND MORE.

STEP INTO YOUR POWER

* Start a wellness journal.
Jot down a few sentences in the morning and evening about how you feel with different kinds of weather, sleep patterns, stress levels, and different kinds of food and hydration. If you're experiencing pain, note what level of discomfort you feel when you wake up in the morning and when you go to bed at night. At the end of the week, note what was helpful and unhelpful.

* Trust yourself. Doctors and other healers are important partners on the path to healing. But like any other humans, doctors aren't always perfect. You are the boss of your body. You know how your body feels more than anyone else does. If any doctor, nurse, or other health professional tells you that your suffering is "all in your head," talk with a trusted adult and seek a second, and third, professional opinion. Practice asking any questions you have before your appointment.

* Educate your loved ones.

Sometimes when we're feeling our worst, the people close to us don't know what to do. Take time to share with your family and best friends how they can help you. Don't be shy about asking a friend to bring you missed homework, or your parents to talk with your teachers if you need extra time, regular bathroom breaks, or other health accommodations.

* Join the party wherever you are.

If you're not able to attend an event or access an activity, remind yourself that "there's always more fun to be had" and ask your friends to Skype or FaceTime, so that you can participate in the action from afar. Catch the silver lining if you're upset about missing out. You now have time for napping, pajama-wearing, video game-playing, TV marathons, pet-cuddling and daydreaming while you recover.

* Be present for others. If it's your loved one who is sick, listen deeply, ask how you can help, and simply say, "I'm here for you, what can I do to support you?" Some people may be too tired to think about what they need, so offer to help bring them meals, run errands, watch TV with them, or simply to be a listening ear.

* Be proactive. Work with your teachers and guidance counselor at school to create a plan for you to get notes, homework, and updates when and if you have to miss school or arrive late because you're sick. If you know what triggers flare-ups, consider making plans that might help, like going to bed early, eating foods you digest well, or taking a relaxing bath on the night before a big test, presentation, or sporting event.

* Be gentle with yourself. Carry small versions of the creature comforts you need with you in case you are away from home when you're feeling ill.

* Kindly set boundaries without apology. If you have special requirements, it's no one's business but yours and the people entrusted with your care. You can choose to explain why you might need an allergy-free lunch, a wheelchair-accessible desk, audiobooks, or a voice-recorder for note-taking in class, but that's your decision. Practice saying: "I appreciate your interest, but it's a personal matter."

* Let it go. I'll never forget how mortified I was when I threw up in the classroom in front of my classmates. When I returned to school, I learned that most people were worried about me and simply wanted to know that I was okay. Be gentle with yourself, and remember that everyone gets sick or knows someone who has been sick. People will forget as soon as Beyoncé drops a new album or something else big happens.

* Have hope. Together with your trusted adults, you will find a routine of care that works for you. Find small things that help when you're feeling run down. Maybe that's a cup of tea, warm blankets, or a hot-water bottle.

FIND THE LESSON

bounce back from the dumps, failures, and other bummers

Do you ever struggle with catching the silver lining in the aftermath of a let-down? When hurt, hardship, and sorrow come my way, I imagine myself as a tree in a field over the course of four seasons.

As I envisage the elements that might impact the tree through sunny days, windy storms, winter chills, and even broken branches, I hark back to the fact that a tree is still a tree in any kind of weather. When the fruits of the tree fall to the ground, I picture the seeds returning to the earth, and sprouting into blooms as a result of time and nourishment.

My go-to daydream reminds me of the first time I heard author and activist Glennon Melton Doyle's motto, **"First the pain, then the rising."** I met Glennon during a time when my broken heart needed mending and I received her words as a soothing-but-forceful call to action, and a reminder that we as humans are as resilient as my imaginary tree.

AT SOME POINT DURING OUR LIFETIME THE CLIMATE MAY BE HARSH DUE TO ELEMENTS WITHIN OR OUTSIDE OF OUR CONTROL. DESPITE THIS, WE HAVE THE ABILITY TO FACE OUR DIFFICULTIES HEAD-ON, TO NURTURE OURSELVES WHEN WE'RE HURTING, AND TO GAIN STRENGTH AND WISDOM TO HELP GET US THROUGH THE NEXT TIME CHANGING WINDS BLOW THE LEAVES OFF OUR STURDY BRANCHES.

STEP INTO YOUR POWER

A helpful way to move past our challenges is to face them, live through them, and accept the lessons they offer as an opportunity to grow. It's okay to acknowledge our disappointment and grief. It's a necessary part of processing our experiences and helps set the stage for us to release, reflect, and rebuild as we turn the page on our pain to start our next chapter.

To be clear, accepting that something is a drag and that it impacted us, doesn't mean that it defines us or limits us from new opportunities in the future. It simply means that we are owning our experiences and their effect on us, and making a decision to learn about who we are, and who we want to be moving forward.

Think about a major hurdle you have overcome. Write down three things you learned about yourself during your time of difficulty. How did you show up at home, at school, and with the people you care about? Would you have done anything differently now with time and perspective? How did you feel in your body during this time? Is there anything you've learned that you will use to nurture yourself in the face of future adversity?

Imagine a four-year-old version of yourself telling an older version of you that they made a mistake and feel sad. Speak aloud what you would tell them. Notice the tone of voice and words you are using, and think about what it would be like if you talked to yourself with the same tenderness and compassion.

Sometimes rejection is protection from what you thought you desired but may not have been the ideal fit. Think about something you really wanted that didn't work out. Were there positive things that later came through for you as a result of one door closing?

SHINE BRIGHTLY WITHOUT BURNING OUT

Do you ever feel like there are not enough hours in the day to get everything done? If so, it's time to take stock of your priorities and determine how to make the most of the time you have. In our fast-paced, performance-driven culture, there's pressure to fill every moment of our day in the pursuit of success. Throughout our lives, from the classroom to the sports field, we're often taught to place more value on our accomplishments, than developing who we are and focusing on our wellbeing.

Growing up, I often felt spread thin after a week overflowing with schoolwork, ballet classes, gymnastics practice, music lessons, Girl Scouts, swim team, and several other projects. Although I enjoyed doing so many different things, I wish I could have spent more time relaxing and rejuvenating, and focusing on the interests and activities that inspired me the most.

While being our best self is an important part of growing as a person, it's important to remember that our inborn worth is not measured by the work we do, or the accolades we get. When we start with a baseline understanding that we are—and always will be—enough, it's easier to protect our energy, use our time mindfully, and make decisions that help us thrive instead of breaking down.

"EVERYONE'S LIFE IS LIKE A CANDLE," JENNIFER, MY CHINESE MEDICINE DOCTOR ONCE TOLD ME. "SOME PEOPLE ARE BORN WITH VERY TALL CANDLES THAT BURN OUT IF THE FLAMES ARE LEFT CARELESSLY UNATTENDED, AND OTHERS MAY HAVE A SMALLER CANDLE THAT LASTS LONGER IF THE FIRE IS PROTECTED.

YOU MAY HAVE A
SMALLER CANDLE
BECAUSE OF YOUR
ALLERGIES AND
CHRONIC ILLNESSES,

BUT HOW YOU
DEFEND AND
HONOR YOUR
LIGHT IS UP
TO YOU."

◎ STEP INTO YOUR POWER

SEE THE MENTAL AND PHYSICAL SIGNS OF BURNOUT CREEPING UP? HERE'S HOW TO COURSE-CORRECT.

* Know the signs. Changes in sleep patterns, appetite, energy level, mood, and fatigue may indicate that you need to pause, reflect on what matters most to you, and take time to restore. If you notice these symptoms in yourself or a friend, talk to a trustworthy adult about getting support and resources.

* Be you. Some people gain energy by being around a lot of people, or filling their days with lots of hands-on engagement, while others need time alone to reflect, restore, and replenish their energy. It's perfectly normal to be either an introvert, an extrovert, or anything in between— but it's important to know what you need to be your truest and brightest self.

* **Honor your time.** Write down your schedule for each week in a planner or on a blank piece of paper. Assign one hour per day as "me time" that is reserved for something that nourishes you or gives you joy. It's up to you how you use your hour, but I suggest honoring your free time by making it a device-free, peaceful time where you're writing, resting, exercising, walking, or creating art.

* **Speak up.** You have nothing to prove to anyone about your worth. I'm here to tell you that you belong. You are accepted, as you are. Anything else, is extra. There's no shame in not being perfect, asking for help, or needing support. Practice asking someone for help this week by kindly telling them what you need—without apology. If it helps, write them a note before you make your request in person.

DEALING WITH DIFFICULT TIMES

TRANSITIONS:
Read your way to presence
and a new perspective

LONELINESS

**HEALTHY
COMMUNICATIONS**

**COMMUNICATING
BOUNDARIES**

TRANSITIONS

"TOMORROW IS TOMORROW. FUTURE CARES HAVE FUTURE CURES, AND WE MUST MIND TODAY."

—Sophocles, *Antigone*

We often think we need to learn something new or do something more to heal discomfort, hurt and grief. I've found freedom, joy, growth, and sometimes even discomfort in the awareness that the practice of unlearning what no longer serves or supports our healing is just as essential.

When I unpacked a dusty box of my old diaries, mixtapes (my generation's playlists), and scrapbooks during a recent trip to my childhood home, I reflected on my gratitude for the past and all the lessons I've learned along the way. I marveled at each object as if it was new. These objects represented a realization that helped me grow.

Read Your Way to Presence and a New Perspective

Much of what I understood about the past evolved due to the triumphs and hardships these pieces represented in material form. It turns out that just like me, my precious objects had been through a lot of highs and lows due to shifts that were often beyond their control, and yet they, like me, were and are still here. They made it and they have meaning. I thought to myself, "I made it and I matter. As do my memories and what I do to evolve because of them."

Some items reminded me of my resilience as a human. I thought this as I read a note on the back of my ninth-grade graduation photo with an indiscernible facial rash that took multiple doctors a long time to solve. At the time, I railed when some well-meaning adults said, "this too shall pass," and dismissed my sadness and shame that I was the target of some rude schoolyard jokes and would forever be enshrined in the yearbook with a face full of spots. And yet, despite

the absolute validity of my pain and my truth at that moment, I did eventually heal and grow. So much so that I now smile when I see that I showed up for that photo despite the almost unbearable anxiety I felt that day. I somehow got myself out of the bed and hopped onto the school bus after begging and pleading to my mom to let me call in sick.

"I understand and want to hear how you feel, but it doesn't mean that these painful feelings or fears are more powerful than you are. Are you going to let some little spots take away your power or are you going

⊙ STEP INTO YOUR POWER

CHANGE IS THE ONLY CONSTANT, AND YET IT IS OFTEN HARD. ARE YOU GOING THROUGH A TRANSITION? HERE ARE SOME ACTIVITIES I USE TO HELP ME COPE:

* **Create!** United States Poet Laureate Joy Harjo said, "What often follows periods of decay and destruction, and chaos is rebuilding and renaissance—periods of fresh invention in thought and art. That's what often emerges from the ruins. You see little plants like after a fire ... coming up from the char." Reflect on these words, read them aloud, and close your eyes. What do you believe is the role of creativity, expression, and art in times of crisis in your life? What would you like to see emerge from a challenge or obstacle you're processing, and how might writing, music, or another way of expressing your creativity help you release and transform?

to learn that the only way out is through? Now, keep your head up and keep it moving." She advised me to read books about others who went through adversity and moved through it so that I would know that I wasn't alone.

Because of her advice, I was able to forgive myself for feeling ashamed of the range of painful emotions that came with the rash. I have since learned to pay attention to the little things and that includes the teachings we've observed directly and indirectly from people who care for and support us.

* **Book it**. After my mother passed away, I began to read her loving notes and inspiring thoughts in the pages of books she had given to me. Although I'm sad that she isn't physically here, I revisit her lessons and find new insights in the books she chose with intention throughout the stages of my life. My experience is that we don't move on, but we do move forward after hard things happen. I'm still grieving, and I always will be, but I have a new relationship to the loss. Through these notes, I learned about her, and the ideas, passions, and inspiration she sought to share with me. Think of someone you care about deeply and a book that you might want to share with them. Draw a picture of the book and write a note you might leave for them on the front page. What has the text you have chosen taught you about being present with your struggles, addressing them, and moving forward?

LONELINESS

What assumptions do people tend to make about you? How do they make you feel? For me, I can recall the annoying frequency of being typecast as both being self-interested and perpetually "lonely" as an only or single child. Frankly, being perceived and labeled as being isolated, forlorn, or distant caused me to feel the ache of loneliness more than the solitary nature of being my parents' only child ever did.

Although I delighted in the love and care I received from my parents, I was raised to make sure that the widespread stereotype about single children wasn't true. Sometimes I overextended myself and devoted too much energy in trying to prove this. I documented what I saw and heard to heal the tender void of feeling outside of the circle.

If I could create words, songs, poems or drawings, then I knew that the world that I had within would be a friend and comfort no matter what. For me, my imagination and self-expression through creativity was the bridge I needed to make bonds with others outside of our home.

Behind the outgoing and confident exterior layer of myself was an occasionally shy and nervous introvert who felt like a misfit for being an only child. I soothed feelings of aloneness by writing myself into existence on my own terms and taking a sense of ownership about the differences that sometimes made me feel apart from others, even in the most crowded rooms. I realized that loneliness was a part of the path of my life, but not the entirety of its definition.

Sometimes I was the only single child, other times, I was the only new kid, the only Black girl; in some other cases, I was the only kid with a disability, the only girl in the brass section of the band, the only American, the only expat student when I returned to the states, the only kid who didn't yet speak or understand our new community's language, and the only fill-in-the-blank in many spaces and places. For me, loneliness could be literal in terms of missing connection and meaningful contact with others, but often it felt like a struggle to belong in places where I found myself coloring outside of the lines even when I tried hard to play by the so-called rules. There is no shame in feeling lonely. Loneliness is like every other human experience and that there is no one way to experience it, heal it, or address it, but one thing is true, we don't have to bear it alone.

Whether your loneliness is due to a big transition in your life, family changes, being othered, grief, illness, social distancing, being distant from your loved ones, friend break ups, a feeling of being left out, rejected, or left behind, or everything else in between, you are not alone, and help is available.

If you're feeling disconnection (whether it is with other people present or without) and you need support visit www.crisistextline.org wherever you are in the world to talk with someone.

STEP INTO YOUR POWER

Learn about how to address loneliness when it knocks on your door. Here are some activities you might find helpful:

* Express yourself

Take a moment to release what you're feeling. Sometimes loneliness is confusing and hard for us to understand or speak up about. Write down what you are feeling and trust the way it comes out. You could even try writing a haiku, drawing a picture, making a list, or leaving yourself a voice memo about what is coming up for you.

* Write to someone who has passed on

I write letters to my late mother whenever I miss her. One of my friends writes letters to her favorite deceased artist who she imagined would have been her best friend. Read *The Diary of Anne Frank* to see the enduring power of letters to a friend during extraordinary crisis and loneliness.

* Be the change and help someone

"Learning to stand in somebody else's shoes, to see through their eyes, that's how peace begins. And it's up to you to make that happen. Empathy is a quality of character that can change the world."—Barack Obama.

Pay it forward and reach out to someone else. Although grief is complex and not something we can "fix," the ability to be a kind and generous force in other people's lives makes me feel less helpless and more empowered.

* Connect With Your Crew

We live in an exciting time where there are virtual and in-person groups for just about every idea, interest, or hobby. Take an opportunity to make new connections with likeminded people in safe and parent/guardian approved way by exploring a new activity. Whether you like languages, music, dance, gaming, reading, writing, sports, or more, there are accessible virtual ways to learn something new and gain a new perspective.

HEALTHY COMMUNICATIONS

Have you ever found yourself saying "yes" to keep the peace instead of staying true to your own needs and feelings? How did it feel in your body? Did you feel seen, cared for, and heard? Now, envision yourself saying with a clear and honest voice what you emotionally and physically need to thrive.

My family raised me to be a curious and compassionate child, but sometimes my upbringing and empathic spirit, led me to be an A+ people pleaser and conflict avoider. Despite my desire to read about independent and outspoken girls in books, I often absorbed both intentional and unconscious messages about automatic deference from my school, family, southern American culture, church, and beloved sitcoms. Also, I sometimes experienced pushback or accusations of being "too much" when I spoke my mind. I realized being perceived as an agreeable and "easy-going" girl was sometimes prioritized and rewarded over telling the truth.

Where did I learn to feel guilty about talking about my real feelings and needs? We live in a culture where we're too regularly taught to always respond with "fine" or "great" when asked how we are. Instead of sharing if we need support, or if we even have the capacity to fulfill a request, we're encouraged to abide by

terms other people set, before taking stock of what we need or feel.

When I tried to recall my first experience of that dynamic, I remember being told off for "rudely" refusing to hug an older male family friend who made me feel uncomfortable. In that moment, although I didn't want to consent to embracing someone I didn't know, I felt ashamed that I was perceived by his partner and some other adults as snobbish and naughty. Now, I am aware that I had every right to set limits about my body and my choices about who to bring close and who to keep my distance from. In fact, I know it is compassionate, clear, and honest to let the people in my life know what I need to feel comfortable and safe, in order to build and foster trust between us. That's why I appreciate when others share their hopes, needs, and growing edges with me in kind.

While communications and practices vary depending on our background and beliefs, respect is a widely held virtue that we should extend to others and ourselves. "Treat others how you want to be treated" is a principle that has many names and manifestations in a variety of languages, traditions, and approaches to life. Since I am aware that our communications style and strength is evolving and always able to be improved with time and practice, I challenge myself to stay kind, curious, and consistent about fostering healthy communications.

STEP INTO YOUR POWER

* Ask open-ended questions This allows us to deeply listen and show genuine interest in someone else's point of view. Practice asking questions that ask why/what/how/tell me more/what do you think about ... Do this instead of leading or closed questions that may be unintentionally biased or based on assumptions. Think about the difference between telling your friend, "You're moving?! Aren't you worried about moving to a new school before the semester?" and "I heard your family is moving. How do you feel about changing schools?" Write down two leading questions and rephrase them as open-ended questions.

* Consider the context If you need to have difficult or courageous conversation, consider asking the other party to speak in person or on a video call instead of texting. As humans, we also communicate through our body language and it is helpful to see and respond to others' cues. This helps us build trust and express empathy during sensitive moments.

* Use "I" statements Be as clear and direct as possible when you speak with others. Instead of saying, "You made me sad" consider saying "I feel sad when you yell at me". Modeling this style of communication moves us away from

assuming full intent and opens the door to allow others to own their actions and statements without shame or blame.

* Be mindful of your body language Studies show that humans place a lot of focus on nonverbal communication, body language, and tone of voice instead of the literal words when we're talking to someone. Since many cultures attach different meanings to eye contact, specific gestures, postures, and movements, it is helpful to listen, observe, and stay curious about what nonverbal messages you're giving and receiving within a specific context. For example, for some cultures, a thumbs up is a positive gesture and in others it is considered offensive.

* Script it up Write a mini script about an interaction you had with someone where you wish you could reauthor the narrative? What would it look like for you to reset the dynamic between you to include more open and respectful communication?

* Viva la resistance Have you ever felt the urge to personalize someone else's unkind reaction or feedback after you expressed your truth? What if you embraced that their behavior had everything to do with them, and nothing to do with you? What are some affirmations you might say to yourself to step into your power despite potential pushback? For example, "I define who I am. I am enough. Their words are theirs and not mine to own".

COMMUNICATING BOUNDARIES

Throughout my life, I have reimagined and replayed many instances where I wished I said no but chose a half-hearted or fear-driven yes to avoid conflict or loneliness. But when I think of the experiences that helped me grow, made me feel firm in my backbone and purpose, and helped me expand my sense of personal integrity, I know that learning to express my limits was actually a way of expressing my freedom.

Some people are experts at respectfully setting boundaries. Others might struggle and feel that it is easier to deny their feelings because they fear being left out, disliked, invalidated, or punished for genuine emotions, feelings, or experiences. When I first started setting boundaries, I noticed some people in my life pushing back or making insensitive comments. Over time, I began to understand that many people who haven't been taught to respect their boundaries, may feel uncomfortable when they see you claiming your personal power. But it is not your problem if they can't understand that your kind and well-defined statement of what respect looks, sounds, and feels like is a thoughtful act and an investment in healthy communication. No matter how others perceive your boundary setting, remember that considerately identifying and voicing your terms and limits is powerful and essential to our growth.

BOUNDARIES PROTECT US AND KEEP US SAFE.

Boundaries help release us from potential future resentment. Every time we set a respectful boundary that honors and expresses what we need to feel emotionally and physically safe in any situation, we open the door to modeling and fostering more integrity and resilience. Even though it can be tough to face our fears of being rejected or criticized, beautiful boundaries enable us to nourish ourselves instead of feeling depleted, burned out or trespassed upon. Most of all, establishing our boundaries enables us to show others that we love them enough to show and tell them what we need to be free, because we want them to feel free too.

⬭ STEP INTO YOUR POWER

* Create a checklist

Healthy relationships are shaped by honesty, deep listening, openness, clear boundaries, and respect for each other's feelings beyond our differences. Like any important skill, we improve our interactions with each other every time we engage with intention and compassion. Take a moment and visualize the kind of healthy communication you want to have more of in your life. Whether the communication you're thinking of is inspired by your own life or someone who motivates you, what aspects do you want to see more of in your relationships? Make a list so you can reference it before your next outing with a good friend. Here is what I have on my list:

· Be clear, compassionate, and consistent.

· Ask how they prefer to be communicated with. Model by clearly and honestly expressing your own preferences: I prefer text and email to set up calls and video chats at another time. I like to plan my calls versus receiving spontaneous phone calls. It helps me stay focused and present.

· Be authentic and open-hearted. Be kind but be firm.

· Use "I" statements. Listen. Try not to project.

· Be curious and ask questions.

· Don't overexplain. "No" is a complete sentence.

· Ask to end the call if it is escalating to an unhealthy place. No yelling.

· Respond vs. React.

· Own your mistakes and apologize. Don't be defensive.

· Be true to your physical needs. Ask for what you need to feel safe and comfortable.

* Protect your energy

Do you have boundaries you'd like to set that focus on how others respect your support, time, or energy?

* Hold yourself accountable

Do you keep boundaries with yourself? If not, be kind to yourself, and keep moving forward. Every day provides us with an opportunity to start again when we have a setback. What is a boundary you will keep with yourself today? For example, I let my loved ones know that I need uninterrupted writing time each day in advance. My quiet time is sacred and when others see how seriously I take it, they usually follow suit.

* Don't be lost for words

Sometimes in the moment it can be hard to stay true to your boundaries and stick to what will serve you best. Jot down five boundary statements to keep with you to remind you that you will never be lost for words when you need them. Here are some of the concise phrases I keep close when I need them:

o Thanks for your input but I am clear about my decision.

o I hear you but I am sticking to my plan.

o No.

o I said no. No is my final answer.

o I don't feel comfortable with this direction/decision/conversation/treatment/dynamic/tone.

o I hear you but I am not OK with how you are speaking to/treating me. I am removing myself from this discussion.

o I don't feel safe in this conversation/engagement/relationship.

o I need to take some time and distance. I'll let you know when and if I'm ready to restart this conversation.

o If this continues, I will stop this conversation.

o If you can't respect my boundary, I do not feel comfortable participating.

INDEX

FURTHER READING

Seeking further inspiration? Consider these resources as you continue to step into your power:

Books

Dear Ijeawele, or A Feminist Manifesto in Fifteen Suggestions,
by Chimamanda Ngozi Adichie

This Book Will Help You Change the World,
by Sue Turton

Little Leaders: Bold Women in Black History,
by Vashti Harrison

The Good Immigrant,
by Nikesh Shukla

Slay in your Lane,
by Yomi Adegoke

Girl Up,
by Laura Bates

Brit(ish),
by Afua Hirsch

You Have the Right to Remain Fat,
by Virgie Tovar

The Girl Guide,
by Marawa Ibrahim

Dare to Be Kind: How Extraordinary Compassion Can Transform Our World,
by Lizzie Velasquez

#NotYourPrincess,
by Lisa Charleyboy

Rookie Yearbook Three,
by Tavi Gevinson

I Am Malala,
by Malala Yousafzai

Demystifying Disability,
by Emily Ladau

Quiet Power,
by Susan Cain

This Book Is Feminist,
by Jamia Wilson

A Bigger Picture,
by Vanessa Nakate

Girls Resist,
by KaeLyn Rich

The Power Book, by
Claire Saunders, Georgia
Amson-Bradshaw, Minna
Salami, Mik Scarlet, and
Hazel Songhurst

Online Resources

Crisis Text Line offers free round-the-clock support to all people experiencing any kind of crisis via text. https://crisistextline.org/

Teen Life offers non-judgmental adult-supervised peer-to-peer support and resources. https://www.teenline.org/

Mindfulness for Teens offers free guided meditations, app access, and book recommendations to help you thrive and manage stress. https://www.mindfulnessforteens.com/

Peer Health Exchange educates young people about healthy decision-making. https://www.peerhealthexchange.org/resources

Films

Own The Room

Maiden Trip

He Named Me Malala

Wadjda

If You Build it

I Am Greta

John Lewis: Good Trouble

Bully

Girl Rising

Brimming with creative inspiration, how-to projects, and useful
information to enrich your everyday life, Quarto is a favourite
destination for those pursuing their interests and passions. Visit our
site and dig deeper with our books into your area of interest:
Quarto Creates, Quarto Cooks, Quarto Homes, Quarto Lives,
Quarto Drives, Quarto Explores, Quarto Gifts, or Quarto Kids.

Step into My Power © 2022 Quarto Publishing plc. Text © 2022 Jamia Wilson.
Illustrations © 2022 Andrea Pippins.

First published in 2022 by Frances Lincoln Children's Books,
an imprint of The Quarto Group.
100 Cummings Center, Suite 265D, Beverly, MA 01915, USA.
T +1 978-282-9590 F +1 078-283-2742   www.Quarto.com

A CIP record for this book is available from the Library of Congress.

ISBN 978-0-7112-7649-9

The illustrations were created digitally
Set in Futura and Grouch BT

Published by Georgia Amson-Bradshaw
Designed by Karissa Santos and Vanessa Lovegrove
Edited by Claire Grace and Katy Flint
Production by Dawn Cameron

Manufactured in Guangdong, China TT052022
9 8 7 6 5 4 3 2 1